PAPER
POEMS

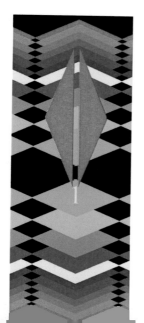

PAPER POEMS

Stefanie Zammit-Raichura

Cover Art:
"Paper Kite", by Aruna Khanzada

Lay out and editing by
My Red Bag
www,myredbag.uk

CONTENTS

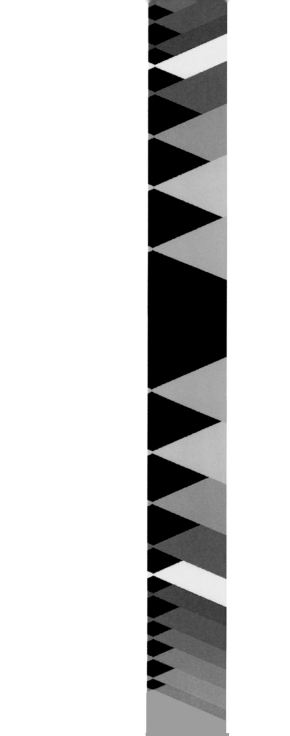

Dreams, they are just that

To sleep with eyes and compromise
Is cause of great confusion;
For truth be told amidst such lies,
Unwise is such this fusion.

As in the dark, and during day,
Such things so oft' are seen;
and though vivid both to so portray,
Some visions just not what they seem.

The sun: reflective of reality,
While dusk: a symbol of a close
Of windows – eyes that cannot see
And a mind that no longer knows.

Along with the stars, they're sleepy rise,
Each face-to-face this fact:
At pillow all must realize
That dreams…

They are just that.

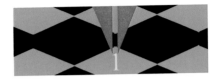

Live Performance

Private party,
Members only.
Wine and dance
And such romance –
Together euphoric,
Euphoric and lonely.

Cold and blue,
As old and new
Harmoniously grieve of wonder.

Man is not welcome
Where man is essential:
Necessity the sole invite
Tonight.

Time keeping: such waltzes
In threes.
Simple and compound,
Odds paired and gliding...

...and one man,
Where man unwelcome,
One man plays host
To the ghosts of guests.

Chasing each other,
Coy yet complacent,
So childishly mature:
A melody that slurs
Drunkenly to delicious coda.
All eyes
Where eyes forbidden,
They stare,
Each stare hidden,
At one man:

Their God.

He twitches in schizophrenic obsession.

Racist for they sit categorically
With their own.
Uniformed and unified,
Molested by man together.
They are struck
Beaten
Whipped
Smothered...

Until they bleed crescendo'ed praises
To their epileptic God.

At last,
When the final wind dies,
The audience stand, aroused.

Their God turns. And bows.

Like a Kite

Winged and weathered,
Full of hope I embark
On new life, on new flight.
Up and up to soar where I
Have always fallen before,
Always skidded on air...
Like a kite.

And I'm disillusioned by
A power that provokes you
To hold my reins, to try choke
My spirit, my life, my throat.
But I smile and I fly
And I surf the whole sky
Knowing well you hold nothing but rope.

Like a kite, set me free!
Drug me stupid – high as a kite!
And when I've had my fill,
And you're emptier still,
Let me down, let me drown here tonight.

Reel me in, faster, pilot!
Slow me down from the ride.
Clad in red, tail to head,
Tugging lasso, who's guiding
Who?

Like a kite,
I am your triumph!
Your win, your endeavor.
Just as you thought you'd never come down,
Well I'm clever all round.
So you peak and I sneak to new heights.

Let me down, Pilot!
I am dizzy from flight.
Ruffled feathers and windblown.
Strewn without you, free

Like a kite.

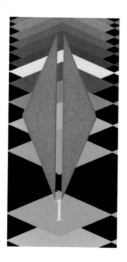

Nostalgic

Nostalgic for my amnesia,
For ignorance is bliss:
When past's ghost is mortal –
A craving just for this.

It's so powerful que j'énvie,
The sorrow of the parting:
To goodbye-kiss the memory –
An end just not worth starting.

I suffer so from nostalgia,
To sit all day and reminisce
The wobbly footprints of time when
Ignorance: it was such bliss!

To deja-vu my amnesia
Of nostalgia's ticking knife:
Which boom-stab-booms growing seizure:
Contagious pools of liquid life.

Like blood exploring humble cloth,
Sucking all the white stuff out –
To bleed and play so I forgot:
Nostalgia for this shadowed doubt.

Jealous of grandfather clock.
Immortal and he never ages.
While I grow more, with every tock,
Nostalgic for the empty pages.

Not a Poem

These words I put to paper,
And whether or not they rhyme,
Aren't composed to seek admiration,
Are just a humble waste of time.

This poem is all but poetry,
Its verses lacking and weak:
A simple message in the through-line,
A pointless game of hide-and-seek.

A child not yet learnt to lie,
A lover's sacrificial song:
One million classes of poetry
Where mine does not belong.

The starving saved from hunger,
Poverty capable, at last, of thrift.
But do not dare to call this poetry –
My talent prizes no such gift.

The sunset from a mountaintop,
A discovery of the unknown.
I am not ignorant: I'll confess
Myself unfit to write a poem.

Peace Breaks Out

Peace breaks out,
Like a plate of China
And detonates to all corners
Of our lives.

Tread on it
And pain will humble you,
And blood remembers again
Of delicacy.

Peace breaks out,
Like a virus.
Consuming territory
Piece by piece.

Contagious,
Incurable and deadly,
And death remembers again
Of caution.

Peace breaks out,
Like a gun exploding,
And bursts the heart
Of some fool.

But who knew
Of that locked and loaded grimace?
And fear remembers again
Of danger.

Peace breaks out,
Like a sudden riot,
And each stranger gets stranger
And stranger

'Till corpses litter the Peace,
Glittering of bravery,
And the Hero remembers again
His place.

Peace breaks out,
Like a plague on both your houses:
The dead and the unborn.

Hopeless we mourn
And hopeless we cry,
While our tears remember again
Of abstinence.

Vigilant.
Let time warn you,
For peace just might break out.

Yes. Forlorn, free,
But look how it tore you!
How it shreds you into
Hope and doubt

Until blood nurtures

The soil it sui-sidled
Into blackmail.

And lest amity grows,
Remember:
Peace will poison
The fight that fails.

Message in a Bottle

The message to the bottle
Is as letters to the page:
Poured or tipped into confidence,
Sealed and so encaged.

Meant for someone secretly,
Too shy and proud to show,
So scribbled silent – heatedly –
Away with them I stow.

Until time has healed my wound,
I lick and push ashore,
Abandon like a castaway: Strewn
Naked on the floor.

Now waiting for significance,
Love and tender care.
Uncork the book: green-bottled since
I ached to proud to share.

Sip and suck, mysterious,
You choose how to behave.
But find me quite delirious:
Bleeding, needing to be saved

From the poison I have drunk,
The bottle of emotion,
The love that I have sunk
Into these words of pure devotion.

Green the bottle – glassy clear –
And red as blood the ink
Which throbs to need you now and here!
Or, broken, it will forever sink.

Buoyant only until pressure
And oxygen are steady.
But fast the ink flows lesser…lesser…
Alas. You were not ready.

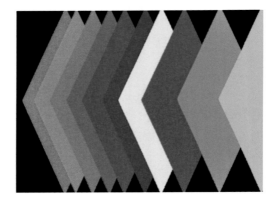

Nothing

Sing songs of nothing to me,
Hum hymns of broken emptiness,
Whisper your sweet nothings to me.
Guilty of nothing: confess.

Shower me with nothingness
And bathe me without water.
Kiss me, but do nothing less
Than Nothing's silent slaughter.

Stab me without battle axe
And hide my body nowhere,
Then pray of nothing over me,
And mourn that nothing's over.

Do this is memory of me,
Scream nothings at my door,
Then bask not in my mystery…
Do nothing. Nothing more.

The Poetry Never Written

If a poem is simplicity,
Humble and angelically
Yearning for life like you;
Tend to poets like one does children,
And weep for those that never grew

And never knew of all the poetry.
For at day's dusk they were smitten-shut
Out of living:
The poems never written – much too
disbelieving
To harmonize from truth to truth.

The Paige who beds the battlefield
Wails messages of woe,
Despising the dust he has bitten,
And the poems never written,
And the love he did not know.

In proud graveyards they shall call to you
In eerie, deathly notes;
That you note all this: the agony
Of poems which they never wrote.

Time stands still in purgatory,
Where, alas, they have no pen;
And here on Earth, Jesus gave us life
That has to end
Before the poetry is written.
And no, you will never be forgiven,
Not for gold nor patriotic spite.

I live time – essential to my need,
Not my duty, nor my right –
But my disgust at your gluttony
And despair for wrongs I did not write.

Human Destruction

Where distant screams haunt the nights,
And streets are filled with empty homes.
Where starving dogs are left to fight
Over lost men's meat and children's bones.

Where a woman's plea comes to an end,
As a sharp gunshot cuts through the air.
It becomes a normal act just to pretend-
To convince oneself there's nothing to hear.

When the world grows silent
And the candle melts the last wax folds.
And we're I'm left in cold confinement
Left only to tear at my bloodstained clothes.

When the hope burns out
And the last cinder dies.
The world's left with only doubts
Where all you hear are endless lies.

When the air is filled with the stench of death
And the dark blood stains the roads.
And the only choice that now is left:
Is a choice of which no one knows.

When the smoke of burning men fills the air:
A smoke that no wind can fend.
When you take a breath and you declare:
This is when it really ends.

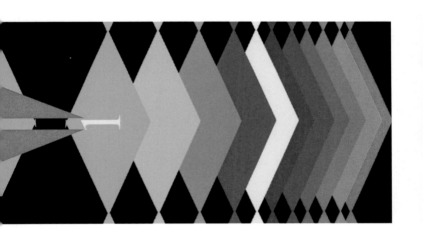

Lightning Source UK Ltd.
Milton Keynes UK
UKRC020248030619
343637UK00010B/174